A Note
Mary Pope Osb

D0468862

MAGIC TREE HOUSE®

[FACT TRACKERS]

When I write Magic Tree House® adventures, I love including facts about the times and places Jack and Annie visit. But when readers finish these adventures, I want them to learn even more. So that's why my husband, Will, and my sister, Natalie Pope Boyce, and I write a series of nonfiction books that are companions to the fiction titles in the Magic Tree House® series. We call these books Fact Trackers because we love to track the facts! Whether we're researching dinosaurs, pyramids, Pilgrims, sea monsters, or cobras, we're always amazed at how wondrous and surprising the real world is. We want you to experience the same wonder we do—so get out your pencils and notebooks and hit the trail with us. You can be a Magic Tree House® Fact Tracker, too!

Here's what kids, parents, and teachers have to say about the Magic Tree House® Fact Trackers:

"They are so good. I can't wait for the next one. All I can say for now is prepare to be amazed!" —Alexander N.

"I have read every Magic Tree House book there is. The [Fact Trackers] are a thrilling way to get more information about the special events in the story." —John R.

"These are fascinating nonfiction books that enhance the magical time-traveling adventures of Jack and Annie. I love these books, especially *American Revolution*. I was learning so much, and I didn't even know it!" —Tori Beth S.

"[They] are an excellent 'behind-the-scenes' look at what the [Magic Tree House fiction] has started in your imagination! You can't buy one without the other; they are such a complement to one another." —Erika N., mom

"Magic Tree House [Fact Trackers] took my children on a journey from Frog Creek, Pennsylvania, to so many significant historical events! The detailed manuals are a remarkable addition to the classic fiction Magic Tree House books we adore!" —Jenny S., mom

"[They] are very useful tools in my classroom, as they allow for students to be part of the planning process. Together, we find facts in the [Fact Trackers] to extend the learning introduced in the fictional companions. Researching and planning classroom activities, such as our class Olympics based on facts found in *Ancient Greece and the Olympics*, help create a genuine love for learning!" —Paula H., teacher

**Magic Tree House®
Fact Tracker**

SOCCER

A nonfiction companion to
Magic Tree House® #52:
Soccer on Sunday

by Mary Pope Osborne
and Natalie Pope Boyce

illustrated by Sal Murdocca

A STEPPING STONE BOOK™
Random House 🏠 New York

The Magic Tree House Fact Tracker series was formerly known as the Magic
Tree House Research Guide series.

Visit us on the Web!
SteppingStonesBooks.com
MagicTreeHouse.com

Educators and librarians, for a variety of teaching tools, visit us at
RHTeachersLibrarians.com

Library of Congress Cataloging-in-Publication Data
Osborne, Mary Pope.
Soccer / Mary Pope Osborne and Natalie Pope Boyce ;
illustrated by Sal Murdocca.
p. cm. — (Magic tree house fact tracker)
Summary: "A nonfiction companion to Magic Tree House #52:
Soccer on Sunday." —Provided by publisher.
ISBN 978-0-385-38629-6 (trade) — ISBN 978-0-385-38630-2 (lib. bdg.) —
ISBN 978-0-385-38631-9 (ebook)
1. Soccer — Juvenile literature. I. Title.
GV943.25.O74 2014 796.334—dc23 2013043648

Printed in the United States of America
10 9 8 7 6 5 4 3 2 1

5571 5261
08/14

This book has been officially leveled by using the F&P Text Level Gradient™
Leveling System.

For Owen Landolf, a really great kid

Soccer Consultant:

JESSIE McMANMON COONEY, soccer player for College of the Holy Cross and coach and board member of the Great Barrington, Massachusetts, soccer league

Education Consultant:

HEIDI JOHNSON, language acquisition and science education specialist, Bisbee, Arizona

Special thanks to Peter Boyce, and the wonderful folks at Random House: Mallory Loehr, Paula Sadler, Jenna Lettice, Heather Palisi, and of course, the intrepid Diane Landolf, who goes where few dare to tread

SOCCER

Contents

Dear Readers,

In <u>Soccer on Sunday</u>, we had an adventure in Mexico City during the 1970 World Cup. We learned what a thrill it is to watch soccer stars like Pelé. We also discovered why soccer is the most popular sport in the world: it's a great game!

In the World Cup, teams from all over the planet compete to see which team is the best. The games are an amazing way for people from different cultures to get to know one another. The World Cup games are so exciting that billions of people watch and cheer on their favorite teams.

What really surprised us is that games like soccer have been around for so long.

Over 4,000 years ago, the ancient Chinese played a ball game that is very much like soccer today.

Soccer teaches people to be good sports and to work hard for a goal. (Get it?) We came away from that World Cup in Mexico City with an incredible feeling about all the players and fans.

Grab your cleats and your soccer balls, and let's head to the field! We've got a game to play!

Jack
Annie

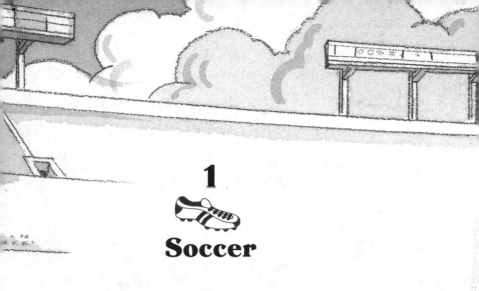

1

Soccer

Soccer is the most popular sport on the planet! There are billions of soccer fans around the world. More people watch the World Cup Finals on TV than the Olympics or the Super Bowl. About three billion people watched the 2010 World Cup in South Africa. That's almost half the people in the world!

People don't just watch soccer—they also play it. Over 260 million people compete on soccer fields everywhere, and it's the number one sport for kids. The stars of tomorrow are the kids practicing their soccer skills today.

 These fans went all out to support Brazil in the 2006 World Cup.

The Fans

Soccer fans often travel a long way from home to watch their favorite teams. They burst into the stadium wearing clothes in their team colors. Some paint their bodies and faces and wave flags and banners.

It's loud in the stands! Fans blow horns, chant, whistle, stamp, sing, and yell at the

Fans blew noisy horns called <u>vuvuzelas</u> during the 2010 World Cup in South Africa.

top of their lungs. The sound can damage their ears.

People feel so strongly about soccer that fights sometimes break out among fans of different teams. Although it doesn't happen often, soccer players have been attacked by fans angry at the way a match ended.

In 1969, a hundred-hour war called the Football War began between El Salvador and Honduras. And it all started at a soccer game!

The Beginning

Girls and women had their own <u>tsu chu</u> teams.

There was no one person who invented soccer. The roots of games like it go far back in history. Over 4,000 years ago, the Chinese invented a game called *tsu chu*, which means *kick ball*. Two teams kicked

16

leather balls filled with feathers and hair into nets hanging between bamboo poles.

The Japanese created a ball game called *kemari*. They still play *kemari*

<u>Kemari</u> players wear hats called crow hats, which make them look as if they're wearing crows on their heads.

today much the way it was played more than a thousand years ago. Players try to keep a ball in the air using only their elbows, head, knees, and back.

Ancient Greeks and Romans also enjoyed ball games. Roman soldiers played with coconuts they brought back from Africa!

In the Acropolis Museum in Athens, Greece, there is a very old piece of pottery showing an athlete balancing a ball on his thigh. It looks so much like a modern soccer player that the image is on the European Championship trophy.

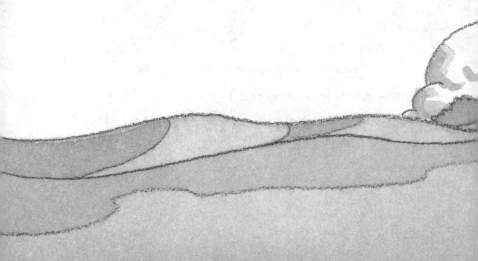

England and Scotland

Soccer as we know it today began in England and Scotland. Hundreds of years ago, people there played ball games without many rules. The games were often violent. Sometimes whole villages played one another, usually on special days before Easter. The goals could be miles apart!

Balls were pig bladders covered in leather.

These early games were called football, but they were not much like soccer games today. Players could grab the ball and run with it. They also kicked, bit, tripped, punched, and even stabbed their opponents. One eyewitness said it was more like a war than a sporting event.

<u>Opponents</u> are people who compete against one another.

Over the years, English and Scottish kings tried to stop the games. In 1314,

King Edward II of England heard that his soldiers were playing ball games instead of practicing archery. To get them back to work and to stop the bloodshed, the king made a law against all football games.

A hundred years later, King James I of Scotland had the same problem. He was so furious that he made a law that said "Na man play at the fute-ball!" (No man shall play football!)

In spite of everything, the games continued. Workers met for matches after work. Rich kids played them in school, and poor kids kicked balls down narrow city streets.

Everyone played by different rules. In some cases, players could hold the ball as they ran. In other games, they could only kick it.

The Football Association

By the nineteenth century, some Englishmen who'd played football games at their private schools formed teams so that thcy could keep playing.

In 1863, they created the Football Association to make sure that everyone played by the same set of rules. Today there are seventeen soccer rules that every good player knows by heart. These rules are called the Laws of the Game.

FIFA

Everywhere the British went, they played soccer. Because they traveled the world, the game began to spread.

By the late 1800s, people in Africa, South America, Europe, and New Zealand held soccer matches. Then teams from different countries began holding

This photograph of an English forward is from 1895.

matches against each other. Around the same time, professional soccer teams were created.

In 1904, FIFA (the Fédération Internationale de Football Association) was created. Its job is to manage professional soccer games around the world and to enforce soccer rules. Today FIFA is in charge of the World Cup.

Football or Soccer?

Why is it called *soccer* in the United States, Canada, and sometimes Australia, while it's called *football* in the United Kingdom, Ireland, and many other countries?

Years ago, when teams started playing under British Football Association rules, players called them Assoc (A-sock) rules. The word *soccer* became a nickname for *association*. The term caught on in

Country
Portugal and Brazil ___
Japan ___
Germany ___
Spanish-speaking
countries ___
Korea ___

countries that have a different sport called
football.

Word

_____ Futebol

_____ Sakka

_____ Fussball

_____ Fútbol

_____ Chukku

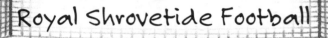

Royal Shrovetide Football

Forty-seven days before Easter is Shrove Tuesday. Every Shrove Tuesday and the day after, men in the village of Ashbourne, in Derbyshire, England, play a game that's been around for over 800 years. It's called the Royal Shrovetide Football Match.

Men who live north of the village stream are on one team. Those who live south are on the other. Play on both days begins at two in the afternoon and lasts until ten at night.

When a special leather ball is tossed in the air, the game is on! Teams try to move the ball to the goal by forming a "hug" and pushing against each other. The goals are three miles apart!

There are very few rules. Players struggle over fields, across streams and rivers, and down the village streets. Shopkeepers board up their stores to keep the hug from crashing into their windows!

2

The Laws of the Game

Soccer is a fast, exciting sport. The aim of a soccer match is for one team to kick the ball into the other team's goal. The team with the most goals wins.

Players must follow the Laws of the Game set up in 1863. To understand a soccer game, it's important to know the rules.

Three referees make sure players obey all the rules. A head referee covers the whole field, while two linesmen watch the sidelines. In soccer, rule breaking is called a foul.

One of the most important rules is that, except for the goalkeeper, players cannot touch the ball with their hands or arms. But they can use their feet, head, or chest to move the ball.

Soccer matches last ninety minutes

Players need to be in shape to last this long. They usually run about six miles during a game.

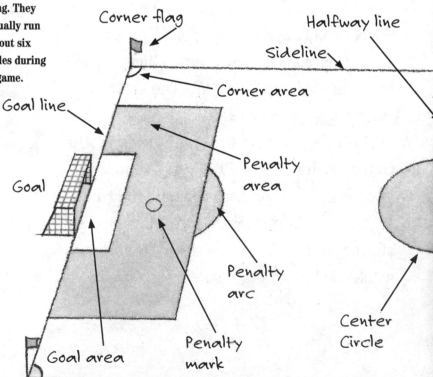

Corner flag

Halfway line

Sideline

Corner area

Goal line

Penalty area

Goal

Penalty arc

Goal area

Penalty mark

Center Circle

with a fifteen-minute break in the middle.
This makes two forty-five-minute halves.

The Field

Soccer fields, or pitches, are always rect-
angles, longer on the sides than at the
ends. The size varies, but all fields have
certain things in common.

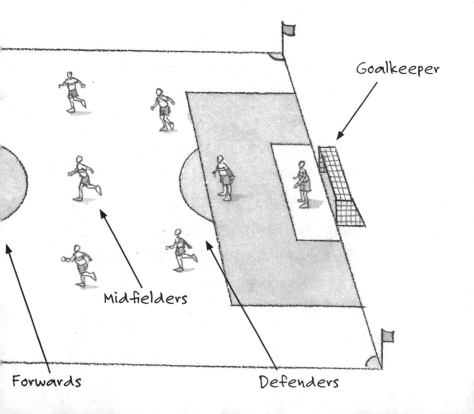

Goalkeeper

Midfielders

Forwards

Defenders

Teams

Kids' games can have fewer players on the field.

Eleven members of each soccer team play at one time. Ten of them cover the field. The eleventh player is the goalkeeper, or goalie, who usually stays in the goal area.

The team that has the ball is on *offense.* The team without the ball is on *defense.*

Besides goalie, there are three basic positions: defenders, midfielders, and forwards.

Defenders protect the goal and keep the other team from scoring. They block shots and try to take the ball from the other team.

Midfielders are the link between the defenders and the forwards. Their job is to keep control of the ball and to try to pass it to the forwards. Midfielders cover a lot of the field, so they do the most running.

Forwards try to score. Great forwards

have amazing skills. Cristiano Ronaldo is one of the best. He once moved the ball past five defenders to score a forty-yard shot to the goal!

Ronaldo is famous for a trick called the step over. As he's dribbling, he moves his foot over the ball as if he's turning in that direction. Instead, he fools the other players by taking off in the opposite direction. No one can ever figure out exactly where he's going!

Ronaldo fools an opponent in a game against FC Bayern Munich, a top German team.

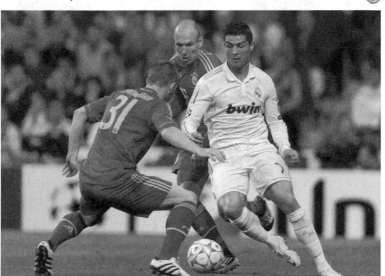

Goalkeepers

Goalkeepers defend the goal. They are the only players who can touch the ball with their hands. Even goalies can hold the ball for only six seconds and only in their own penalty area.

Goalies block shots by catching the ball, kicking it, or punching it away.

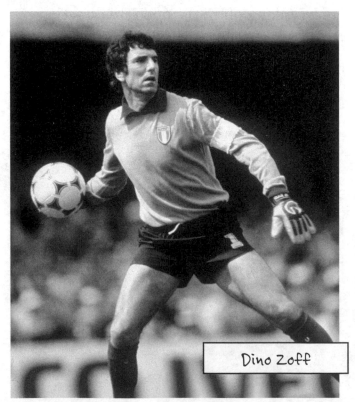

Dino Zoff

It would be hard for any goalie to beat Dino Zoff's all-time record. From September 1972 to June 1974, he played a total of 1,142 minutes in international matches without allowing a single goal!

Goalies can also score goals. Rogério Ceni has scored over one hundred, the most of any goalkeeper.

Rogério Ceni

Out of Bounds

When a ball crosses one of the sidelines or goal lines, play stops. The team that touched the ball last loses control of it. Depending on where the ball went out of bounds, play restarts in different ways.

Throw-Ins

If the ball goes over a sideline, a member of the team that did not last touch the ball gets a throw-in. The player stands outside the sideline at the point where the ball went out of bounds. She throws the ball over her head with both hands. Both of her feet must stay on the ground as she throws. This is the only time a field player can touch the ball with her hands.

Goal Kicks and Corner Kicks

If a player on offense sends the ball over the goal line, play restarts with a goal kick. The ball can be placed anywhere in the goal box.

Usually the goalie or one of the defenders kicks it back into play.

If a player on defense puts the ball out of bounds over the goal line, there's a corner kick. The ball is placed at the corner on the side of the field where it went out. A member of the team on offense kicks it toward the goal.

Because the ball lines up with the goalpost, it's very hard to score a goal right from a corner kick. Players often jump up and try to head the ball into the goal after a corner kick.

Free Kicks

Under the rules of soccer, after a foul is called, play stops, and the other team gets a *free kick*.

For a free kick, the ball is kicked closest to the spot where the foul took place.

The referee has two cards to notify players about fouls.

A yellow card is a warning, so watch it!

A red card means it's a serious foul. Off the field!

There are two types of free kicks. For less serious fouls, like touching the ball twice in a restart, the other team takes an *indirect kick*. The referee places the ball on the spot where the foul happened. The player kicks it to a teammate. Another player must touch the ball before it can go into the goal.

If the foul is a penalty foul, such as kicking, hitting, or pushing, the other team gets a *direct kick*. This means that the player taking the kick can aim straight for the goal.

The ball is placed on the penalty mark, about twelve yards in front of the goal.

Penalty Kicks

When a defending team makes a penalty foul in its penalty area, the other team takes a free shot called a penalty kick. Only the goalkeeper stands between the ball and the goal.

A player gets ready for a penalty kick in the 2013 FA Youth Cup.

Because the kicker is so close to the goal, the ball can reach the net at a speed of 125 miles per hour!

Soccer players follow strict rules about fouls and free kicks to keep matches safe and fair. In fact, the Laws of the Game cover nearly everything—the shape of the field, the uniforms, and how the game is played. People might say that "soccer rules," but every soccer player knows that "the rules rule."

43

Women's Soccer

During the 1920s in the United States and England, women played soccer for fun and exercise. One match in England attracted over 50,000 people!

In 1921, England's Football Association decided that soccer was not a safe sport for women. They banned all women's matches on Football Association soccer fields. The ban wasn't lifted until fifty years later!

In the 1970s, soccer became a popular sport for women and girls. Talented players began playing in schools and colleges and even on professional soccer teams.

Today women compete in the Olympics and in matches around the world. The Women's World Cup began in 1991. Thousands watched as the United States beat Norway. There are over 29 million girls and women playing soccer worldwide.

3

Let the Game Begin!

People don't need fancy equipment to play soccer. All that's needed is a place to play, friends to play with, a ball, and something to mark the goals.

Soccer players wear shorts and shirts with their names and numbers on them. They strap on shin guards under long socks to protect their legs. Soccer cleats, or shoes, have rubber spikes on the bottom to prevent slipping.

Goalies wear shorts and long-sleeved padded shirts. Their shirts are often bright colors so they can be easily seen.

 Jorge Campos, from Mexico, was famous for wearing a wild mixture of zigzag stripes in brilliant colors.

Unlike field players, goalies wear special gloves to protect their hands and help them grip the ball.

Goalies usually wear the number 1.

kickoff

The Kickoff

Every game starts with a kickoff. Before the match, the referee tosses a coin

After a kickoff, Vuk Bakic of Serbia scored a goal two seconds into the game.

in the air. The team that wins the toss chooses which goal to attack for the first half. The other team kicks off. The team that has won the toss kicks off for the second half.

When the kickoff begins, each team is on its half of the field. The referee puts the ball down on the center mark. A kicker and one teammate stand in the center circle. No other player can enter it until the ball rolls forward one complete time.

Then the kicker taps the ball to her teammate, who will try to pass it back to someone on their team. The kicker is not allowed to touch the ball again until someone else has touched it.

The soccer game has begun! Now the other team can try to steal the ball.

Whenever there's a goal, a kickoff restarts the game. The team that didn't score gets to kick off.

Turn the page to read more about soccer skills.

Soccer Skills

Ball control is everything in soccer. Skillful players move the ball around the field and try to score. Players have a hard time

Jack and Annie's Soccer Skills Exhibition

Dribbling

Running while tapping the ball lightly from the inside of one foot to the other is called dribbling.

Practice dribbling without looking at the ball!

Trapping helps me control it!

Trapping

Use your foot to stop the ball, pointing your heel down.

aiming the ball if they kick it with their toes, so good soccer players practice other ways of kicking. Here are some of the most important soccer skills.

Shooting

When you're going for a goal, try kicking the ball with your laces. This lifts the ball off the ground and sends it sailing through the air!

> He shoots! He scores!

> I plant one foot and kick with the inside of the other foot. This is a push pass.

Push Pass

The fastest way to move the ball up the field is to pass it to a teammate.

Headers

Headers are a way of using the head to shoot, block a shot, pass, or steal the ball from the other team. Players hit the ball with the middle of their forehead. Headers can injure a player if they're not done correctly or if the player is too young. Kids under twelve should never try them!

The longest header goal was made by Norway's Jone Samuelsen. It went over 190 feet!

Skill in Action

One of the best passers in the world is Xavier (shahv-ee-AIR) "Xavi" Hernández Creus, from Spain.

Even though Xavi most often kicks short passes, he's also great at long, powerful shots. Like all professional players, he kicks with both feet and changes direction in an instant.

Xavi says that he's always looking for an open space so that he can pass the ball.

In a game with the French team Paris Saint-Germain, Xavi passed a total of ninety-six times!

Cristiano Ronaldo is famous for more than just the step over. He kicks the toughest free kick of all, called a knuckleball. A knuckleball makes the ball zigzag at a slow spin all the way to the goal. The goalkeeper can't predict where it will land.

Scientists have researched how the knuckleball works. They say the trick is kicking the ball at just the right speed. Ronaldo worked for years on his knuckle-ball and says he never stops practicing.

Diego Maradona

Diego Maradona, from Argentina, is known as the best dribbler ever. He called his dribble the Gambetta. The Gambetta looks a lot like a dance from Argentina called the tango.

Players change directions over 1,000 times during a game.

Maradona would pretend to move one way and then quickly and gracefully change directions. There are great videos online of Maradona in the 1986 World Cup as he dribbles past half of the English team.

People call soccer the beautiful game. It's both a game and an art. The art comes after years of practicing basic skills over and over. Long hours of practice can make the most difficult moves seem easy and even really beautiful.

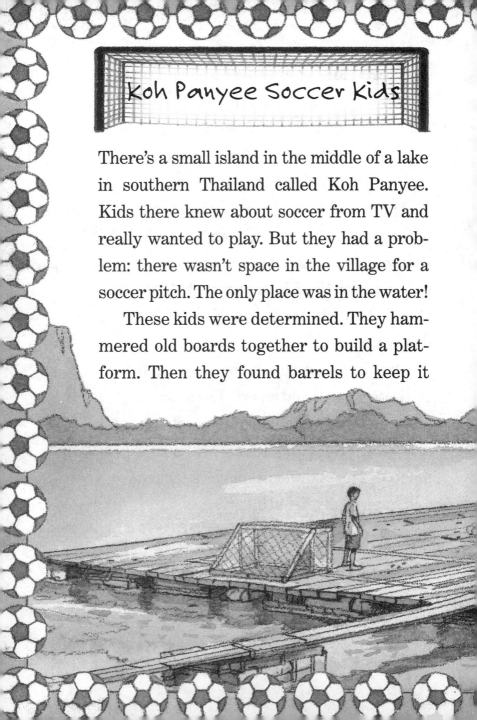

Koh Panyee Soccer Kids

There's a small island in the middle of a lake in southern Thailand called Koh Panyee. Kids there knew about soccer from TV and really wanted to play. But they had a problem: there wasn't space in the village for a soccer pitch. The only place was in the water!

These kids were determined. They hammered old boards together to build a platform. Then they found barrels to keep it afloat. When they finished, they had a floating wooden soccer field! But the platform was rough and wet and not very big. Kids and balls kept tumbling into the water. Because the players had to be really accurate or they'd wind up in the water, they learned to play well—really well.

The Koh Panyee soccer team began winning all kinds of tournaments. They were the number one youth club in all of Thailand from 2004 to 2010!

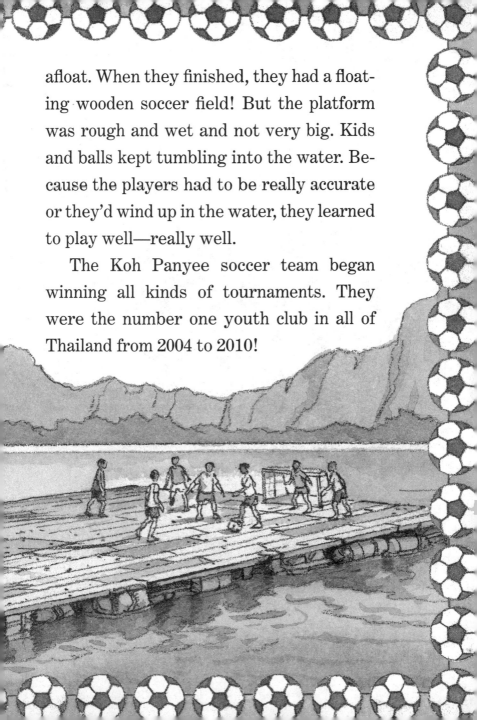

4

Great Players

Dr. Robbie Wilson at the University of Queensland in Australia wanted to know what makes a great soccer player. His studies showed that the best players have natural talents like endurance, speed, and the ability to make fast decisions.

But his research also showed that great soccer players have outstanding skills from hours and hours of practice. So even if a kid isn't the fastest player on the team, practice can make him or her a top player.

Pelé the Great

Pelé may be the greatest of all soccer players. When he was born in Brazil in 1940, his parents named him Edson Arantes do Nascimento. His friends later called him Pelé. Pelé says that neither he nor his friends know why they called him that. It just happened.

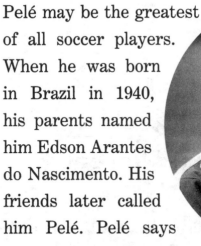

Pelé was named after Thomas Edison, the inventor of the electric light.

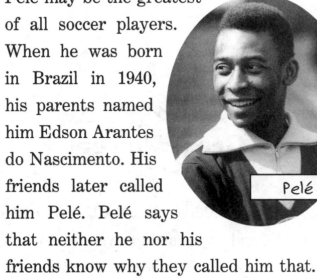

Pelé

Pelé's father, Dondinho, was a retired soccer player. He began training Pelé when he was very young. The family was poor, so the boy made soccer balls from old socks stuffed with newspapers. Pelé and his friends played soccer barefoot in the dusty city streets. People called the ragged boys the barefoot team.

After Pelé's teacher caught him playing soccer when he should have been in class, Pelé dropped out of school. He got a job on the streets shining shoes. When he was eleven, Pelé bought his first soccer shoes and a real ball. It was clear to everyone that he had true soccer talent.

Santos, one of Brazil's top professional soccer teams, heard about the promising young player and hired Pelé when he was only sixteen. The team made a fantastic choice. Pelé became a soccer star, and with his help, Brazil won the World Cup in 1958, 1962, and 1970.

Pelé scored the most amazing goals. One of his specialties was the bicycle kick, which few players have ever mastered.

 In a bicycle kick, Pelé scissored his legs midair to shoot the ball over his head.

Pelé was happiest on the field. He played 1,363 games with a record 1,283 goals. Whenever he scored, he saluted the crowd. Sometimes he bowed to the goalkeeper or shook his hand. Pelé's fans would leap to their feet, chanting his name over and over again.

Pelé was so popular that in 1969, a cease-fire was called in the civil war in Nigeria so that people there could watch him compete in a match.

Pelé played for twenty-two years. Since he retired in 1977, he's traveled the world, teaching kids to take pride in themselves and to make friends by playing the game he loves so much.

Pelé claims that no one is born to be a great soccer player. He says that everything in soccer comes from practice and a deep love of the game.

Now, let's head up the field and meet some other fantastic players!

Abby Wambach

BORN 1980—UNITED STATES

Mary Abigail Wambach was the youngest of seven kids. To keep up with her older brothers, she started playing soccer when she was four. Abby scored so many goals that they put her on a boys' team. In college, Abby was an outstanding player. She moved on to play for the U.S. national team and the Washington Freedom club.

Abby's a powerful player, just under six feet tall. She's famous for her ability to trap balls and her talent as a striker. Abby was outstanding in the FIFA Women's World Cup in 2003, and in 2004 played on the Olympic gold medal team.

Today Abby plays for the Western New York Flash and the U.S. national team, which won the gold medal in the 2012 Olympics. In the same year, she was also the FIFA Women's World Player of the Year. She has scored a record 160 goals in international play, more than any other male or female player! In her free time, Abby hangs out with her English bulldog, Kingston, who rides a skateboard.

David Beckham

BORN 1975—ENGLAND

David Beckham started playing soccer when he was seven. Just seven years later, Manchester United, a famous English team and one of the best in the world, chose him for their youth club. At seventeen, David became a professional midfielder for Manchester United. Later, he played on teams in different countries.

David's specialty was "bending" the ball, or kicking it in a curve. Goalkeepers couldn't tell where it would land. David also knew exactly what was happening all over the field, even if he was right in the middle of the action.

Like Pelé, David played in three World

Cups. He led Manchester United to six Premier League Championships and two Football Association Cups.

David retired in 2013. He now works as a Goodwill Ambassador for the United Nations Children's Fund (UNICEF). He says it's the best job he's ever had.

Mia Hamm

Born 1972—United States

Mia was born with a foot problem. As a child, she had an operation and needed a cast and special shoes. Mia's mother says that when she was three, Mia watched some people playing soccer in the park. She ran after the ball and gave it a good kick!

During her career, Mia played in four Women's World Cups. She was also in the 1996, 2000, and 2004 Olympics. Mia was one of the few women ever chosen by FIFA for the list of greatest living players. She's scored 158 goals—that's more goals in international games than anyone except Abby Wambach.

Mia retired after the 2004 Olympics to

raise a family. Because her beloved brother died of a blood disease, Mia began a foundation to help people with similar diseases.

Ronaldinho

Born 1980—Brazil

Ronaldinho's real name is Ronaldo de Assis Moreira. His teammates called him Ronaldinho, which means *little Ronaldo*. Ronaldinho learned soccer from the men in his family. At thirteen, he made news by scoring twenty-three goals in one game!

Ronaldinho has played as a midfielder and forward for France, Brazil, Spain, and Italy. At the World Cup quarterfinals in 2002, he shot a goal 115 feet from the net!

Ronaldinho is an awesome player. He's especially good at tricking the other team into thinking he's going to make one move and then making another. Ronaldinho is cool under pressure, super skilled, and super fast.

He's been a FIFA Player of the Year twice. Today he's captain of the Brazilian national team and plays for Atlético Mineiro.

Lionel "Leo" Messi

Born 1987—Argentina

Even at five, Leo Messi was a gifted player, and he was an outstanding player on youth teams. But when Leo was eleven, doctors found that his body didn't make enough growth hormone. He needed medicine every day to grow taller.

Leo's family couldn't afford his treatment. The director of the team FC Barcelona in Spain heard about the problem. He offered to pay for everything if Leo and his family moved to Spain so Leo could train there. At thirteen, Leo began playing soccer at the youth academy in Barcelona.

Leo not only grew—he also became one of the best forwards ever. He led teams in

Spain and Argentina to many victories. It's almost impossible to list all of his awards... there are just too many. He has been World Player of the Year four times, and lots of people claim that Leo Messi is the best player in the world today.

Iker Casillas

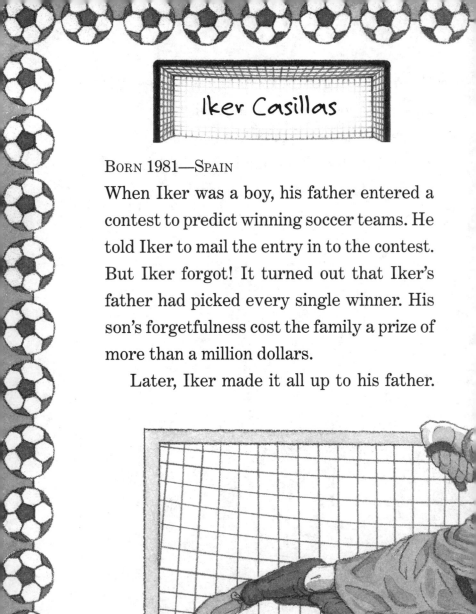

BORN 1981—SPAIN

When Iker was a boy, his father entered a contest to predict winning soccer teams. He told Iker to mail the entry in to the contest. But Iker forgot! It turned out that Iker's father had picked every single winner. His son's forgetfulness cost the family a prize of more than a million dollars.

Later, Iker made it all up to his father.

He became one of the best goalies in history. He plays for Real Madrid and the Spanish national team. As captain, he led Spain to win its first-ever World Cup! Iker has won the European Footballer of the Year award twice.

Iker is one of very few players to win all major team and championship finals. The boy who lost a million now makes many millions as one of the greatest goalkeepers the sport has ever seen.

Michel Platini

BORN 1955—FRANCE

At sixteen, Michel Platini tried out for the French club Metz and didn't make it because of injuries. Metz gave him another chance. But this time he really blew it! While taking a breathing test, he fainted. Doctors thought his heart was weak and told him never to play again.

But Michel didn't give up and was signed by a small French team. In one match, he impressed everyone by scoring a hat trick. A hat trick is scoring three goals in a game.

Michel later joined the Italian club Juventus. In 1983, he scored sixteen goals and was European Footballer of the Year. In the European Championships in 1984, he

played for France and scored nine goals in five days. It was France's first international championship.

When Michel retired in 1987, he became president of the Union of European Football Associations.

Wayne Rooney

Born 1985—England

Wayne Rooney's dream was to play soccer for Liverpool's Everton team. When Wayne was nine, he scored ninety-nine goals in one season! A scout from Everton watched him and was really impressed.

Everton chose him for its youth team. By sixteen, Wayne had made it to the adult team. At that time, he was the youngest player ever to score in a professional English football league.

In 2004, Wayne began playing for Manchester United. In his first game, he scored a hat trick!

Whether he's a striker or a midfielder, Wayne is one of the best players in the

world. He has scored over 200 goals for Manchester United and is the English national team's fifth-highest scorer ever.

Wayne is also known for his quick temper and has had his share of red cards. He says he constantly works on controlling himself.

Every night before a big game, Wayne has a ritual: before he falls asleep, he thinks of all the ways he can beat the goalie the next day. Sometimes he thinks of so many ways, he can hardly sleep!

5

The World Cup

Every four years, thirty-two teams from around the world compete in the World Cup. Each country chooses its best professional players to be on its national team. Players must be citizens of the country they play for. Leo Messi, for example, played in the 2010 World Cup for Argentina, even though he plays professionally in Spain.

Two hundred countries hold matches in hopes of making it to the World Cup. FIFA picks the top thirty-one teams to take part. The thirty-second team is always from the country where the event will take place.

FIFA has chosen Brazil to host the 2014 World Cup. The teams will arrive about a month before the championship game. During this time, there will be sixty-four matches in Rio de Janeiro and São Paulo. The two top teams compete for the World Cup trophy.

Excitement

Tens of thousands of people attend the World Cup games. Billions watch on TV. During the 2006 World Cup in Germany, thousands of people gathered every day to watch matches on a giant screen near the gates of the old Berlin Wall.

In a small village in Zambia, people hurried to a school's soccer pitch at night. They watched the 2010 finals on a huge screen set up by UNICEF.

All over the world, people are glued to their television sets. (In poor towns, they crowd around televisions in tiny shops to root for their country's team.) The World Cup rules!

Beginning of the Cup

The World Cup was the dream of a French lawyer named Jules Rimet. Jules became the president of FIFA in 1921. He believed that if countries played soc-

Jules Rimet

cer together, there would be more peace and unity in the world.

Not many people shared Jules's vision. Many countries wanted to control their own games. They also didn't want their teams to be away for the time required to take part in the games. Only thirteen countries agreed to compete.

In 1930, Uruguay, a country in South America, offered to host the games and pay for teams to get there.

No one traveled by air then, and sailing across the ocean took a long time.

Jules boarded a boat to Uruguay with teams from France, Belgium, Romania, and Yugoslavia. Because the trip and the finals took a long time, everyone would be away for two months.

Uruguay won gold medals in soccer in the 1924 and 1928 Olympics.

Jules carried a small statue of Nike, the Greek goddess of victory, for the winning team. Uruguay won the cup, beating Argentina 4–2.

87

The Games Continue

Two more World Cups were played before World War II began in 1939. There were no games in 1942 or 1946. During the war, an Italian football official hid the trophy in a shoe box under his bed.

Brazil hosted the World Cup in 1950 and built the largest soccer stadium ever. The Brazilians felt confident that they would win, but Uruguay took the cup again!

It was a bitter defeat, but Brazil bounced back. It has gone on to win the cup five times, more than any other country.

Pickles and the Trophy

Jules's Nike statue was gold-plated silver with lapis lazuli, a rare blue stone, on it. It was awarded to World Cup winners for forty years.

In 1966, four months before the World Cup in England, a thief stole it! The police searched, but the cup was missing. A week later, a man was walking his dog, Pickles. Pickles started snuffling around

a bundle of newspapers in a hedge near a neighbor's car. Pickles had found the trophy!

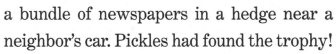

Smile, Pickles!

In 1970, Brazil won the World Cup for the third time and got to keep the trophy forever. But in 1983, someone stole it **again**! It has not been seen since.

The new World Cup trophy shows two winning players holding the world over their heads.

The Trophy Today

A solid gold trophy was created for the 1974 World Cup. The winning team keeps the cup for four years until the next World Cup.

The year and name of the winners are engraved on the bottom. In 2038, there will have to be a new trophy. The current one won't have room for any more names.

Unforgettable World Cup Moments

There are some wild moments in a World Cup that no one will ever forget. For example, in a 1998 game, Cuauhtémoc Blanco, from Mexico, jammed the ball between his feet and jumped past two defenders. This is now known as the Blanco Bounce.

In the 1938 World Cup, Italian soccer legend Giuseppe Meazza was taking a penalty kick when the elastic on his shorts broke. He held on to them with his left hand and kicked. After the kick, his shorts fell down!

In the finals in 2002, Hakan Sükür, from Turkey, scored a goal only eleven seconds after the kickoff! It was the fastest goal ever in a World Cup.

Pelé scored a hat trick at his first World Cup. He was only seventeen. In the 1982 World Cup, László Kiss, from Hungary, scored a hat trick in seven minutes!

An outstanding Italian player, Marco Tardelli, scored two goals in the 1982 World Cup, winning the match against Germany. Marco went ballistic! He ran all over the field, tears streaming down his face, screaming, "Goal! Goal!" It was as if he couldn't believe it! Marco's famous celebration is known as the Tardelli Scream.

The Tardelli Scream

Eight countries have won the World Cup since it began.

Country	Wins
Brazil	5
Italy	4
Germany	3
Argentina	2
Uruguay	2
England	1
France	1
Spain	1

Soccer Connects

The World Cup can bring together countries that are having problems with each other. During the 1998 World Cup, relations between the United States and Iran were very bad. People worried that a game between the two could be angry and even violent.

The exact opposite happened. The two teams posed for pictures with their arms around each other and exchanged gifts. The fans were respectful and enjoyed the match. Iran won the game and the team captains shook hands afterward. It was a great day.

Each Iranian player came onto the pitch carrying white roses. These flowers are a symbol of peace in Iran.

A statue of Jules Rimet stands in his hometown in France. It's placed on a grassy spot that looks like a soccer penalty area. When people pass by, many remember the man who began the World Cup in the hope of making the world a more peaceful place.

Turn the page to celebrate the World Cup with us!

Celebrate!

Every time a country wins the World Cup, there are huge celebrations. When Italy won in 1982, the whole country went crazy! People danced and sang in the streets. They climbed up on rooftops and beat on pots and pans and set off fireworks. Crowds surged through the streets chanting and waving Italian flags.

In the ancient city of Rome, fans jumped up and down in the fountains. Foghorns and sirens sounded from the harbor. Boats and cars blasted away on their horns. It was a noisy, wild, and wonderful night that no one who was there will ever forget.

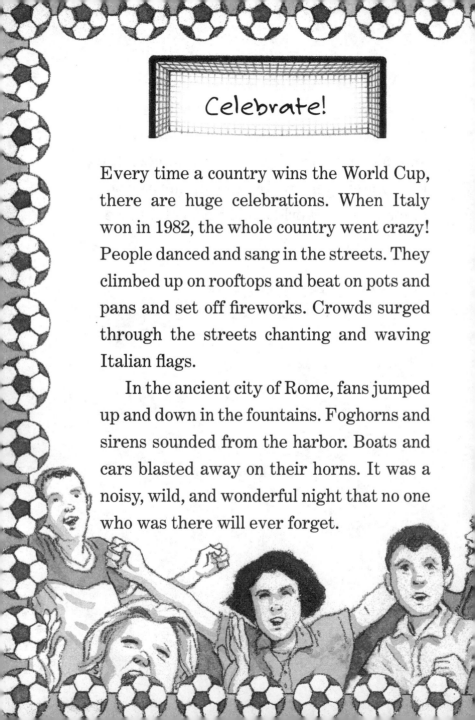

6

Soccer Changes Lives

For children from poor countries, soccer can be more than just a game—it can change their lives. To many kids, owning a soccer ball is just a dream. Like Pelé, they often make balls out of anything they can find. UNICEF works with groups all over the world that use soccer to help kids. They send balls to children who need them.

These groups are setting up soccer schools in poor countries where life is often hard for children. In Liberia, over 6,000 kids are being taught soccer and life skills. Child soldiers in Sudan are learning soccer as a way back to normal life. In Afghanistan, UNICEF has made it possible for kids in refugee camps to play soccer. If the children are playing, they're happier.

Super Balls and the Tiger

Darfur is an area in Sudan, in Africa, suffering from a long civil war. Kids there were playing soccer with balls made out of string and paper.

When word got out, groups around the world donated soccer balls. But after only a few minutes of playing, the rocky soil popped the balls.

Then someone had a bright idea. What if

there were soccer balls that never popped? They came up with one and tested it on a tiger at the Johannesburg Zoo in South Africa.

The tiger usually popped six balls a day. With the new balls, he only burst two! Since then the balls have gotten even stronger.

Today kids in many troubled areas, including Darfur, are playing with these super balls. There are plans to send millions to children everywhere.

Balls That Light Up
Billions of people live without electric lights. They usually use kerosene lamps instead. Fumes from the lamps pollute the air and cause breathing problems.

Now there are special soccer balls that make light! They are called Sockket Balls. Kicking the ball makes energy. While kids kick the balls around, the balls store power for the light. Then kids take them home and have light for reading books and doing homework. Children in ten countries now have Soccket Balls, and more are on the way.

Soccer Teaches

Soccer teaches that good sportsmanship and hard work pay off. Playing can also build confidence and self-control. But one of the best reasons to play soccer is simply to have fun the way Pelé and his friends did. Kids from Afghanistan to Brazil to the United States enjoy the wonderful game of soccer.

It feels good to be outside with friends dribbling and passing and running. And if you really practice, maybe you could become a soccer star just like Pelé.

Doing More Research

There's a lot more you can learn about soccer. The fun of research is seeing how many different sources you can explore.

Books

Most libraries and bookstores have books about soccer.

Here are some things to remember when you're using books for research:

1. You don't have to read the whole book. Check the table of contents and the index to find the topics you're interested in.

2. Write down the name of the book.

When you take notes, make sure you write down the name of the book in your notebook so you can find it again.

3. Never copy exactly from a book.

When you learn something new from a book, put it in your own words.

4. Make sure the book is <u>nonfiction</u>.

Some books tell make-believe stories about soccer. Make-believe stories are called *fiction*. They're fun to read, but not good for research.

Research books have facts and tell true stories. They are called *nonfiction*. A librarian or teacher can help you make sure the books you use for research are nonfiction.

Here are some good nonfiction books
about soccer:

- *The Everything Kids' Soccer Book* by
Deborah W. Crisfield

- *The Flea—The Amazing Story of Leo
Messi* by Michael Part

- *Hope Solo, My Story* (Young Readers'
Edition) by Hope Solo

- *Pelé*, DK Biography series, by James
Buckley Jr.

- *Toward the Goal: The Kaká Story*
by Jeremy V. Jones

- *The World's Greatest Soccer Players*,
Sports Illustrated Kids series, by Matt
Doeden

Museums and Soccer Stadiums

Many museums and soccer stadiums can help you learn more about soccer.

When you go to a museum or stadium:

1. Be sure to take your notebook!
Write down anything that catches your interest. Draw pictures, too!

2. Ask questions.
There are almost always people at museums and soccer stadiums who can help you find what you're looking for.

3. Check the calendar.
Many museums and soccer stadiums have special events and activities just for kids!

Here are some museums and stadiums that will help you get to know soccer:

- Aloha Stadium—hosts Pan-Pacific Championship Games (Honolulu, Hawaii)
- Arrowhead Stadium—old home to Kansas City Wizards and hosts international matches (Missouri)
- CenturyLink Field—home to Seattle Sounders and hosts international matches (Washington)
- Lockhart Stadium—home to Fort Lauderdale Strikers (Florida)

DVDs

There are some great nonfiction DVDs about soccer. As with books, make sure the DVDs you watch for research are nonfiction!

Check your library or video store for these and other nonfiction titles about soccer:

- *All the Right Moves to Beat and Get Past Your Opponent*, with Coach Roby Stahl, from Soccer Learning Systems

- *Backyard Soccer Drills* from Marty Schupak and the Youth Sports Club

- Coerver Fundamentals series, with Wiel Coerver, from Reedswain DVD

- *Soccer for Kids: Getting Started* from Tango Entertainment

The Internet

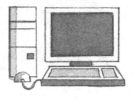

Many websites have lots of facts about soccer. Some also have games and activities that can help make learning about soccer even more fun.

Ask your teacher or your parents to help you find more websites like these:

- biography.com/people/groups/athletes /soccer-players

- ducksters.com/sports/soccer.php

- factmonster.com/sports.html

- fifa.com/worldcup

- zoomwhales.com/themes/sports /soccer.shtml

Good luck!

Index

James I, 22
Japan, 17–18, 26
Johannesburg Zoo,
103
Juventus, 78

kemari, 17–18
kickoffs, 49–51, 92
Kiss, László, 92
knuckleballs, 55–56
Koh Panyee, 58–59
Korea, 26

Laws of the Game,
23, 31–43
Liberia, 102

Manchester United,
68–69, 80–81
Maradona, Diego, 56,
57
Meazza, Giuseppe, 92

Messi, Lionel "Leo,"
74–75, 83
Metz, 78
Mexico, 48, 92
midfielders, 33, 34,
68, 72, 80

New Zealand, 23
Nigeria, 65
Nike, 87, 88
Norway, 45, 54

Olympic Games, 13,
44, 66, 67, 70, 87
out of bounds, 38–40

Paris Saint-Germain,
55
Pelé, 62–65, 68, 92,
101, 106
penalty kicks, 42–43,
92

Photographs courtesy of:

Have you read the adventure that
matches up with this book?

Don't miss Magic Tree House® #52

Soccer on Sunday

Jack and Annie travel to Mexico City for
the 1970 World Cup, where they must
find the final secret of greatness for
Merlin. Thanks to a new friend, Jack and
Annie make it to the stadium just in
time for the big match. But to discover
the secret, Jack and Annie still need to
meet one of soccer's greatest heroes . . .
the legendary player Pelé!

If you liked Magic Tree House® #5:
Night of the Ninjas,
you'll love finding out the facts
behind the fiction in
Magic Tree House®
Fact Tracker

NINJAS AND SAMURAI

A nonfiction companion to
Magic Tree House® #5:
Night of the Ninjas

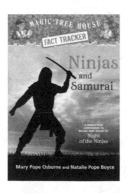

It's Jack and Annie's very own guide
to the mysteries of ninjas and samurai
in ancient Japan.
Coming September 2014!

Magic Tree House® Books

Magic Tree House® Fact Trackers

More Magic Tree House®

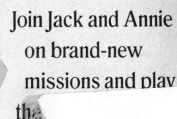
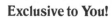